#NotYourPrincess

VOICES OF NATIVE AMERICAN WOMEN

Edited by Lisa Charleyboy and Mary Beth Leatherdale

annick press
toronto + berkeley

Annick Press Ltd.

ONTARIO ARTS COUNCIL
CONSEIL DES ARTS DE L'ONTARIO
an Ontario government agency
un organisme du gouvernement de l'Ontario

We acknowledge the support of the Canada Council for the Arts and the Ontario Arts Council, and the participation of the Government of Canada/la participation du gouvernement du Canada for our publishing activities.

Cataloging in Publication
#NotYourPrincess : voices of Native American women / Mary Beth Leatherdale, Lisa Charleyboy, editors.

Issued in print and electronic formats.
ISBN 978-1-55451-958-3 (hardcover).--ISBN 978-1-55451-957-6 (softcover).--
ISBN 978-1-55451-960-6 (PDF).--ISBN 978-1-55451-959-0 (EPUB)

1. Native women--Canada--Ethnic identity--Juvenile literature.
2. Native women--Canada--Biography--Juvenile literature.
3. Indian women--North America--Ethnic identity--Juvenile literature.
4. Indian women--North America--Biography--Juvenile literature. I. Leatherdale, Mary Beth, editor II. Charleyboy, Lisa, editor III. Title: #Not your princess.
IV. Title: Hashtag not your princess.

E98.W8N68 2017   j971.004'97   C2017-901403-X
                                    C2017-901404-8

Published in the U.S.A. by Annick Press (U.S.) Ltd.
Distributed in Canada by University of Toronto Press.
Distributed in the U.S.A. by Publishers Group West.

Printed in China

annickpress.com
lisacharleyboy.com
marybethleatherdale.com

Also available in e-book format. Please visit www.annickpress.com/ebooks.html for more details.

For every Indigenous woman who has ever been called "Pocahontas" – L.C.

For my mother Hazel with thanks – M.B.L.

I am always trying to escape—from dangerous situations, from racist stereotypes, from environmental destruction in my territory, and from the assault on my freedom as an individual and as part of the Nishnaabeg nation. As an Indigenous person, I have to escape in order to survive, but I don't just escape. I hold this beautiful, rich Indigenous decolonial space inside and around me. I am escaping into Indigenous freedom. I am escaping into Indigenous land and my Indigenous body.

~ Leanne Simpson (Michi Saagiig Nishnaabeg)

RedWoman by Aza E. Abe (Turtle Mountain Ojibwe)

contents

pathfinders

"It seemed as if the spiritual and social tapestry they had created for centuries was unraveling. Everything lost that sacred balance. And ever since, we have been striving to return to the harmony we once had. It has been a difficult task. The odds against us have been formidable. But despite everything that has happened to us, we have never given up and will never give up."

~ Political leader and author Wilma Mankiller (Cherokee Nation, 1945–2010)

I came to terms with what it meant to be an Indigenous woman in my twenties, around the same time as the trial of a male serial killer who targeted vulnerable Indigenous women dominated the news. I was shattered by the very presence of those headlines, because I knew that with one simple twist of fate, I myself could've been listed as one of the victims.

I had spent most of my life up to that point filled with self-loathing and a sense of aimlessness. I hadn't yet realized that the key to finding my direction was directly tied to finding my place—and pride—as an Indigenous woman.

Too often I've seen, we've all seen, those headlines that send shivers down spines, spin stereotypes to soaring heights, and ultimately shame Indigenous women. Yet when I look around me, I see so many bright, talented, ambitious Indigenous women and girls, full of light, laughter, and love.

This book, co-edited with my longtime peer and mentor Mary Beth Leatherdale, gave me the space to not only write a love letter to all young Indigenous women trying to find their way, but also to help dispel those stereotypes so we can collectively move forward to a brighter future for all.

Lisa Charleyboy (Tsilhqot'in – Tsi Del Del First Nation)

Transform by Tania Willard (Secwepemc Nation)

shawl of memory's embrace

Clear Wind Blows Over The Moon *(Cree/Innu-Montagnais/Dene/Métis)*

past

present

future

myriad textures

woven into

the fabric of life

lived

unlived

being

seeing

scene after scene

a shawl of memory's embrace

adorns futures unknown

the ties that bind us

Tear

Linda Hogan (Chickasaw)

I remember the women.
Tonight they walk
out from the shadows
with black dogs,
children, the dark heavy horses,
and worn-out men.

They walk inside me. This blood
is a map of the road between us.
I am why they survived.
The world behind them did not close.
The world before them is still open.
All around me are my ancestors,
my unborn children.

I am the tear between them
and both sides live.

I remember the women.
Tonight they walk
out from the shadows
with black dogs,
children, the dark heavy horses,
and worn-out men.

They walk inside me. This blood
is a map of the road between us.
I am why they survived.
The world behind them did not close.
The world before them is still open.
All around me are my ancestors,
my unborn children.

I am the tear between them
and both sides live.

Artwork by Wakeah Jhane (Comanche/Blackfoot/Kiowa) ————

Blankets of Shame

Maria Campbell (Métis)

Maria Campbell's great-grandmother, whom she called
Cheechum, *was a niece of Gabriel Dumont, a Métis leader.
Her whole family fought beside Louis Riel during the North-
West Resistance at Batoche, Saskatchewan, in 1885. She
shares what her great-grandmother taught her about how
Indigenous people protect themselves from prejudice in
society and the shame that comes with it.*

My *Cheechum* used to tell me that when the government
gives you something, they take all that you have in return—
your pride, your dignity, all the things that make you a living
soul. When they are sure they have everything, they give you
a blanket to cover your shame. She said that the churches—
with their talk about God, the Devil, heaven, and hell—and
residential schools taught children to be ashamed: we're all
a part of that government. When I tried to explain to her that
our teacher said governments were made by the people, she
told me, "It only looks like that from the outside, my girl."

She used to say that all our people wore blankets, each in his
or her own way. Someday, though, she said, people would
throw them away and the whole world would change. When
I got older, I understood about the blanket; I wore one too.
I didn't know where I started to wear it, but the blanket of
shame was there and I didn't know how to throw it away.

But the years of searching, loneliness, and pain are over for
me. *Cheechum* said, "You'll find yourself, and you'll find
brothers and sisters." I have brothers and sisters all over the
country. I no longer need my blanket to survive.

Enrollment by Ka'ila Farrell-Smith (Klamath/Modoc)

two braids

Rosanna Deerchild (Cree)

on my first day
of kindergarten

mama weaves
two braids

so tightly
as if they will never let go

too tight i fuss pull
at my temples

she loosens stitches
spit shines them

into long perfect arrows
wraps and wraps

tips into exclamation
points memories

entwined
of her first day at residential school

of falling wisps of hair
of never going home

mama kisses my forehead
lips a warm berry

on my brown skin

sends me on my way
i wave smile back

my braids bounce
behind me

a reminder of who i am
always pointing me

back home

Illustration by Danielle Daniel (Métis)

My Parents' Pain

"I don't see trauma as a downfall or a weakness. I see it as a lesson and a way to build strength. Through Ceremony I faced myself and saw my pain for what it truly was (intergenerational) and not my or my family's fault. My parents' pain is directly connected to residential schools. I know why my family is fractured. I can't imagine going through what they did. I don't blame them. I was born to them to show them love and to be the love that they never knew or never received."

Madelaine McCallum (Cree/Métis)

#LittleSalmonWoman
Lianne Charlie (Tagé Cho Hudän)
I come from salmon & lattes lodgepole pines & townhouses
fish head soup & Danish pastries

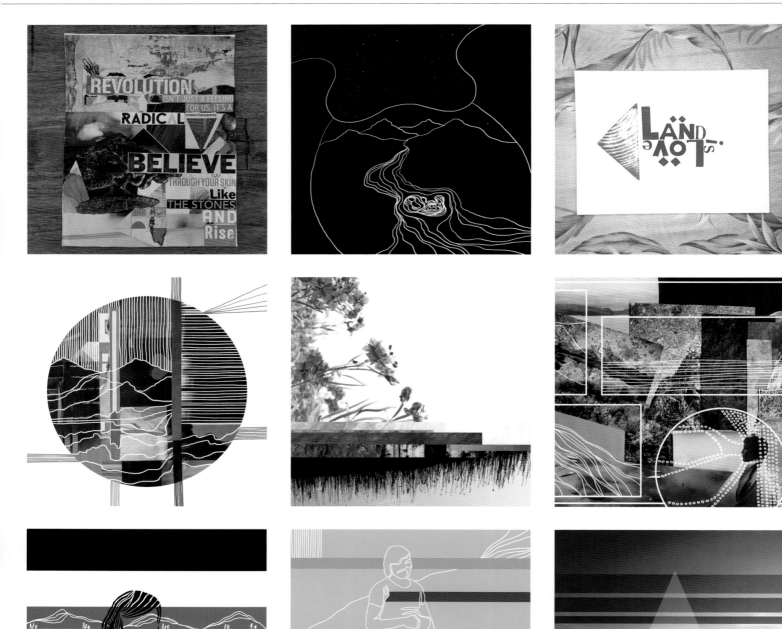

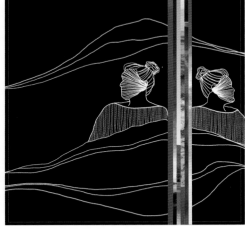

she moves
with love & courage

through the world
of mountains

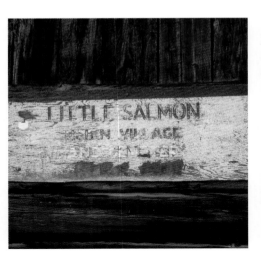

LITTLE SALMON

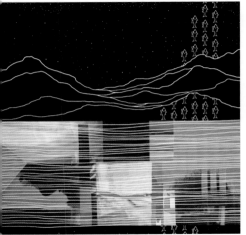

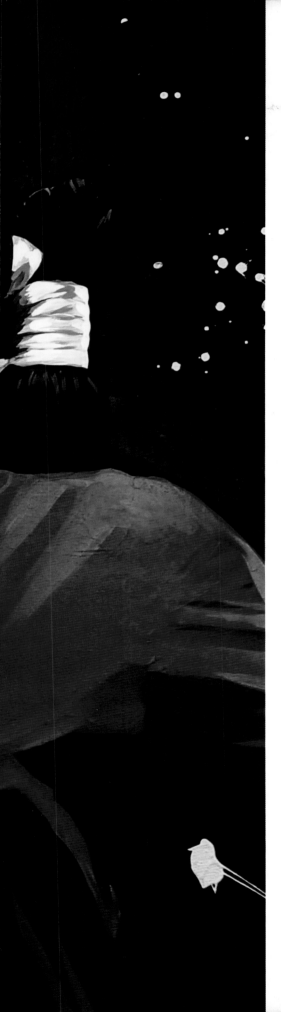

Reclaiming Indigenous Women's Rights

Nahanni Fontaine (Anishinaabe)

For the first twenty years of my life, I had absolutely no sense of what it meant to be an Indigenous woman. I grew up divorced from ancestral cultural teachings and connections. I endured multiple physical, mental, and sexual traumas. I numbed myself with drug and alcohol addictions.

I wasn't alone—my mother before me was taught from very early on to be "white," not allowed to learn Ojibway language and ceremonial teachings.

With the support of family and friends, alongside the wisdom of a trusted healer, I began an amazing journey of self-reclamation, healing, and renewal. I studied both traditional and western knowledges, starting with the question, "What does it mean to be an Indigenous woman?"

Indigenous women have always known and embodied beauty, independence, courage, strength, forgiveness, generosity, resilience, and authenticity. It's important to understand that what we currently believe or are fed as "feminine" characteristics or behaviors are firmly entrenched within the confines of western patriarchy.

Patriarchy is quite simply the systematic oppression and regulation of women's bodies, minds, and spirits. Patriarchy sets the markers and outlines the box of what we can and cannot do; say or cannot say; think or cannot think; express or cannot express; live or cannot live. Western patriarchy very methodically and strategically sought to oppress Indigenous women and girls and diminish their spaces and places, seeing them as disposable, as "less-than."

In Indigenous culture, Indigenous women and girls are sacred, known as life-givers, as independent, as autonomous, as decision-makers. Early explorers, traders, missionaries, and settlers wrote about Indigenous women and girls, describing them as inferior and sexualizing them. There is power in language. Colonizers saw Indigenous women and girls as promiscuous: as whores, as slaves, and as "squaws"—the most degrading word to describe women.

Altering, diminishing, and transforming Indigenous women and girls' spaces and places within the nation, tribe, territory, community, and family has sown and set the seeds and firmly entrenched the conditions for physical and sexual violence; the breakdown of community-based thinking; intergenerational trauma; economic and political marginalization; the regulation and oppression of our reproductive health, including being sterilized by the government without our consent; the theft of our children, taken to residential schools and put up for adoption without our permission; and, ultimately, the theft of our very lives.

When we begin to understand the colonial legacy and its collateral damage to the minds and bodies of Indigenous women, we can begin to forgive, accept, and heal ourselves from the countless hurtful, damaging ways in which this trauma manifests itself. When we embrace our long-standing inner memory of the richness of our teachings, in those moments we reclaim and honor our ancestors' truth, courage, and resilience.

As with our grandmothers and mothers, generations past and present, Indigenous women have deep and intrinsic means of learning to let go and embracing our fears to set forth new paths for ourselves, for our communities, and for our children, always demanding that elusive space of equality.

Resilient by Sierra Edd (Diné)

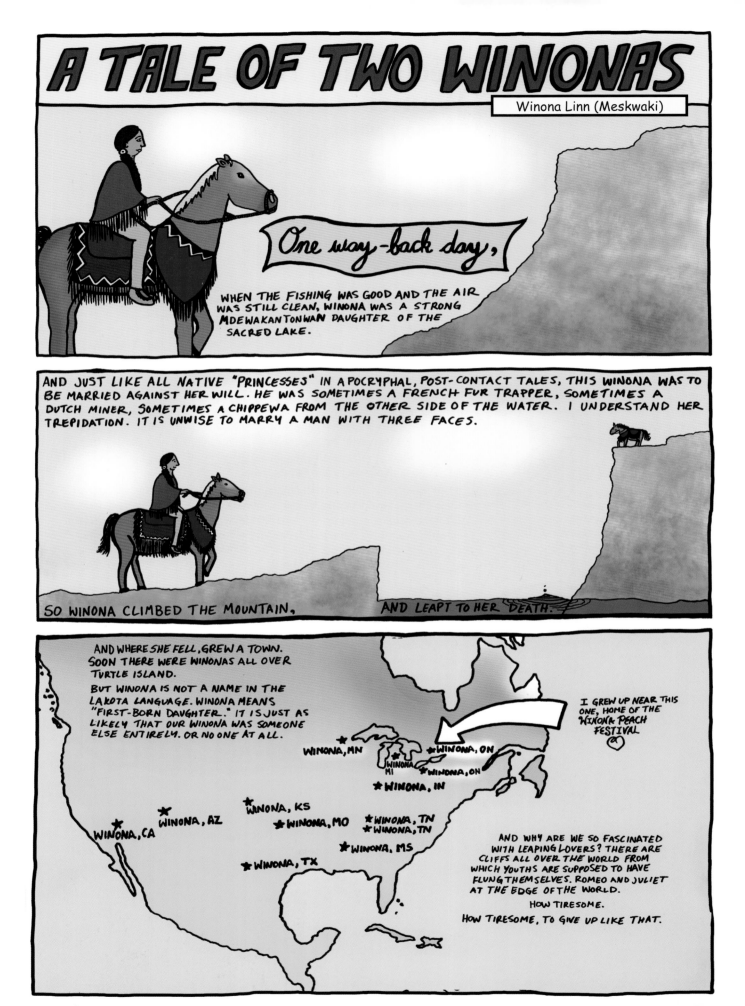

Leaks

Leanne Simpson (Michi Saagiig Nishnaabeg)

dirt road
open windows

beautiful one, too perfect for this world

the immediacy of mosquitoes
humidity choking breath

my beautiful singing bird

five-year-old *gitchidaakwe*
crying silent, petrified tears in the back seat
until the dam finally bursts

*you are the breath over the ice on the lake. you are the one the grandmothers
sing to through the rapids. you are the saved seeds of allies. you are the
space between embraces.*

she's always going to remember this

you are rebellion, resistance, re-imagination

her body will remember

you are dug-up roads, 27-day standoffs, the foil of industry prospectors

she can't speak about it for a year, which is one-sixth of her life

*for every one of your questions there is a story hidden in the skin of the
forest. use them as flint, fodder, love songs, medicine. you are from a place of
unflinching power, the holder of our stories, the one who speaks up.*

the chance for spoken-up words drowned in ambush

you are not a vessel for white settler shame,

even if I am the housing that failed you.

—————— *Tagé Cho (Big River)* by Lianne Marie Leda Charlie (Tagé Cho Hudän)

My Grandmother Sophia

by Saige Mukash (Cree)

My grandmother Sophia passed away. I didn't want to talk about it. I didn't know how to deal with it. I got angry. I got very frustrated with things that I couldn't control. People around me were having dreams and feeling her presence. But I couldn't.

Then I started drawing her. When I worked on it, I felt less frustrated. I felt her presence in me. Everything she taught me. Every memory that I have with her. She is a part of me, my sweetest grandmother Sophia. I never lost her.

I finally finished the drawing. I almost didn't want to. Every time I picked up my pencils, I was letting go.

When I was young and would fall or hurt myself at her house, I remember her arms around me and her kisses on top of my head as she said in Cree, "Kayâ pîkwêyihta. Don't worry. Kika- miywayan. You'll be okay."

I don't ever draw portraits.
But this time it helped me a lot.
She helped me a lot.

The first thing **I am is a person**. **I am a woman**. And I am part of a nation, **the Indian nation**. But people either relate to you as an Indian or as a woman. They relate to you as a category. A lot of people don't realize that **I am not that different** from everyone else.

Winona LaDuke
(Anishinaabe/Ojibwe)

I know **I can survive** anything in life because **my family overcame** so much during assimilation, and my people are still alive and well and my tribe, although **facing challenges**, continues to flourish, just as it has for thousands of years. **My tribe has survived**, and so will I.

Jen VanStrander
(Western Band of Cherokee)

it could have been me

Natanya Ann Pulley (Navajo)

In my mother's world we all fall from cliffs. She points to a sign by an outlook of Canyon De Chelly. It shows a young Indian woman falling from a cliff, her hand clamped to the arm of a soldier as she pulls him down with her. My mom is chatting on her cell phone to a friend about our trip. She pauses and points to the sign and side-says to me, "That could have been you." Goes back to her conversation. I think of all the times falling, the ways. I think she might know. "What?" I ask. Staring at the girl in eternal plummet who pulls her assaulter with her, I look over the side of the cliff. My mom says, "The wind is strong here and that could have been you. Be careful. I rather you be terrified than think," she warns, "that you can beat the wrath of Mother Nature."

Morning Star by Rayna Hernandez (Lakota)

I don't want to be afraid

"All over the news there are Native girls being

hurt and abused. I feel afraid when I walk

around. But I don't want to be afraid.

I want to have good energy."

— *Imajyn Cardinal (Cree/Dene)*

Actress Imajyn Cardinal in **The Saver**

she is riding

JOANNE ARNOTT (MÉTIS)

down through the suburban grey
streets dreamed by developers and
implemented for traffic floes

comes riding the turquoise green Grandmother
riding her mighty Sow
onto the battlefield

down along the highway of decay she rides
between the crack houses and on to piggy palace
where the spirits of the women are lifted

out of the horror, out of the muck, like
troubled teeth and bone fragments
their spirits gather and rise, and rise

all of our dead sisters lifted by those winged women
well-versed in the protocols of the battlefields
recognizing the existence of the battlefields, here

as along the highway of tears

shoulders back
open arms
open chested

the turquoise green grandmother breathes
along with each one of us still traveling
our inner city streets

our turns on the quiet highways
our love affairs gone wrong
our villages overrun

shoulders back
open arms
open chested

letting flow the sounds of the inside
the sounds of our voices calling out songs of sorrow
the sounds of our drums rising through time and through sky
the sounds of our warm bodies traveling swift
through the families
and through the forests

shoulders back
open arms
open chested

we accompany our sisters and brothers to the threshold
we hold them until they are fled, and then
we hold them more

we accompany our mothers and our fathers
we accompany our children, our friends, and o
the many strangers, the star gazers

we hold our dying persons long, dwell
inside memory

we lay each one to rest
slowly

shoulders back
open arms
open chested

tears coursing from the inside
across the outside and wetting
our multihued skins

the touch of a warm palm in passing
through hair on a child's head gently

the touch of a lover to beloved
any where, at any time

the touch of a grandmother's warm palm
on the cheek of her adult offspring

or along the stiff hair on the Sow's back
she is riding

ONTO THE RED ROAD

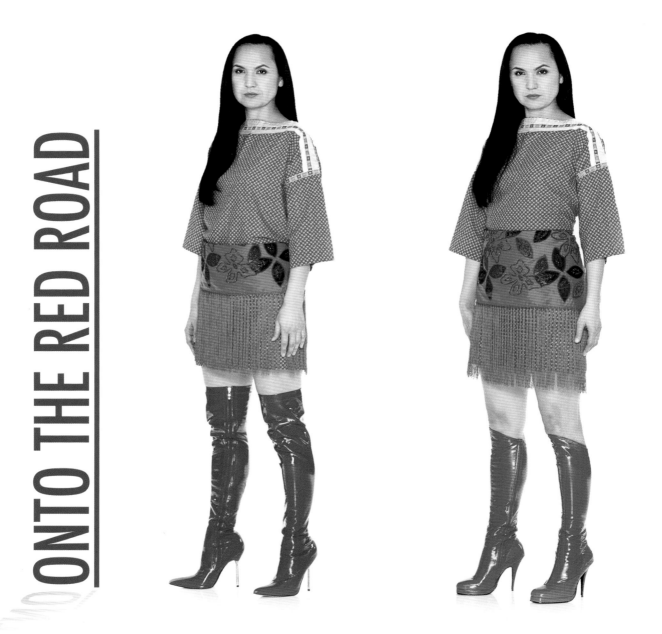

Dana Claxton (Hunkpapa Lakota)

Artist's Statement:

Onto the Red Road is about transformation, spirituality, and objectification of Indigenous *wiyan* ("women" in Lakota). The color *sa* ("red" in Lakota) is a sacred color within the tradition of the Sundance. As the *wiyan* takes her Sundance stance in the fifth image, her clothing becomes more Indigenous, as does her spirituality.

The Things We Taught Our Daughters

Helen Knott (Dane Zaa/Cree)

sometimes we taught them silence
to let the secrets stay on their lips
sometimes we taught them to look away
to forget and not bear witness

we showed them how
to play hide-and-seek
with historical afflictions
to pretend that the monsters from the closet

Didn't escape. Don't exist. Are not real.

sometimes to protect our own wounds
we forced our daughters not to feel
maybe we were taught this ourselves
if you focus hard enough on forgetting
you can live through any kind of hell

Hush. Quiet now. That's enough, my girl.

Silence.

fat lips and bruised eyes
say more than the mouth will tell you
show less than what the eyes have seen

It didn't happen. Forget about it. He didn't mean it.

We don't call the police on our own.
Just learn to stay away . . . Stay away. Stay . . . away.

somewhere we learned how to create an asylum
for the very things
that plague our dreams
somewhere we learned blind eyes and buried skeletons
provide just enough relief
to live just enough
without ever really living

we stuck sexual abuse up on the mantelpiece
picture framed the portrait of rape
and named the old Rez dog domestic dispute
we gave all of this shit a home
the aggressive interloper intrudes
and we accepted its right to exist
love just isn't really love
if he doesn't say it with his fists

Enough now. Quiet. He didn't mean to.
They would never hurt you like that.
Your Uncle, he loves you.

our inaction translating to
another generation
accepting the presence of violations

We were little girls.

we should have slept safely in our beds
mothers should have said
my girl, you are worth a thousand horses
and any man
would give a thousand more
we would know the phrases

Speak up. It is never your fault. No means no.
You have the birthright to be free from harm
and any man who would violate these treaties between bodies
would be dealt with by the women
Because we protect our own
even if this means calling the police on our own.

Because, my girl
You are sacred, valuable, indispensable, and irreplaceable

this is what needs to be said, needs to be shown, and needs to be told
because our daughters will one day grow old
and maybe they'll be women
with short-term memories
practicing daily burial ceremonies
focused on forgetting

it is time to remember
time to summon our voices from the belly of the earth
time to feel, cry, rage, heal, and to truly live life instead
it is time to tell ourselves and our daughters
the things that should have been said

Freedom in the Fog

Zoey Roy (Cree/Dene/Métis)

"Sometimes you have to hit rock bottom before you can rise up."

I left home when I was thirteen. Trouble followed me wherever I went. Erin and Dakota were the only other Native girls in my class. We were inseparable. Their families gave me a place to call home when I didn't have one. They bought me Christmas presents, bailed me out of jail, and bought me school supplies. While I was living with them, I tried to get through grade eight but I didn't make it. I moved to New Brunswick to live with my dad on a military base. I had never lived in an environment that was so structured. I couldn't relate to a lot of the kids in my school or community. But there was a reserve not too far away that I found myself venturing to in my spare time. I babysat for a lady on her bowling nights and saved my money to buy hip-hop CDs. I would memorize the lyrics then perfect the way I delivered them.

I never lasted long with Dad and moved back to Saskatoon. I went to Ave U and 21st to live with my sister, Patricia, who was seventeen, a single mother trying to escape an abusive relationship. Trying to keep a house, to make it a home, to go to school, to take her daughter to daycare. She's only four years older than me but she's always been like a second mom. Every week, she would come to bail me out.

Photos of Zoey Roy by Tenille Campbell
(Dene, English River Nation/Métis) of Sweetmoon Photography.

I was a transient kid. I had no idea what stability meant. I was homeless and I didn't know it. I couldn't get a job, even though I was throwing job applications everywhere. I never did drugs, so I hustled. The time I spent on the streets was fuelled by greed and desperation. I did a lot of things I wasn't proud of. The guilt built up quickly and self-destruction was the easiest outlet. It was easier to give up, to be a statistic, to align with society's desire for me.

After two years on the streets, I found myself in Kilburn Hall, a youth detention center. I was there twenty-eight times over sixteen months, to be exact. I was a fourteen-year-old with a baby face charged with stealing a car or possession of a weapon and I was staying in the same room with people who were charged with murder. I had to stand up for myself when I was in Kilburn. Not a week went by that I wasn't held for gang involvement but I was never in a gang. I was often put in solitary confinement where I was only allowed a blanket, a pillow, a mat for a bed, paper for homework, and a pencil. It was within those confines that I began trying to master the craft of hip-hop.

Going from the police station to the cruiser, to the youth detention centre, to the holding cells, to the courtroom made me acutely aware that it wasn't a coincidence I was there. I take responsibility for the crimes that I've done. But almost everyone who was incarcerated was Aboriginal and everyone who had decision-making power was not. The place was built for us. I didn't want to be a statistic. I decided to rebel against the system and be successful.

It Could Have Been Me

by: Patty Stonefish (LAKOTA)

It could've been me...
It could've been me at 12.

It could've been me at 15.

It could've been me at 18, and 19, and 21.

If things had gone one step further
It could've been me
But my Indigenous Sister whispers in my ear
"Don't you dare stop dancing here."
I will not beat myself up for something
someone else did to me —
that poison is theirs.
I will not succumb to the belief I am tainted —
for I am like steel forged by fire —
adversity has only made me stronger.
I will not believe I am weak —
I know I am indomitable.
I have the privilege of another day.

Honor Song

Gwen Benaway (Anishinaabe/Métis)

Omaamaamiiyan*
come in the dead of night

down sherbourne street
to the girls on the corner

with painted faces,
dollar store makeup

heels and nylons,
sisters of dark

who carry fire
in their ribs

who go missing
meet bad ends

left for dead
discarded lovers

girls like me
break every day

in this great city,
just off the rez

out of the clinic
waiting for hormones

work to survive
a war we can't leave

see us walk fast
past men who shout

hear us pray
to dead grandmothers

burn sweetgrass,
tobacco under moons

by rivers we know
carry our bodies home

every step we take,
everyone we love

we re-create the universe,
daughters of the water

we have not forgotten
the power of being

all of us sing now,
in broken bones

bruised lips,
scarred lungs

taking chances,
beautiful lights

we grow brave
in the absence

of any safe touch,
in our father's rage.

we have nothing,
everything is in us

our love of these
impossible bodies

our faith in this
unbroken sky

our trust of the
infinite universe

our souls to burn
as an offering

to any being
who will listen.

*Omaamaamiiyan means
"the Mother of us all" in
Anishinaabemowin.*

We Are Sacred by Chief Lady Bird (Anishinaabe) ————

Sexualization of **Indigenous women** leaves a **broken spirit**. Young girls are the canary in the mine shaft ... they start killing themselves, it means **future generations** are at stake. And no amount of money will ever rebuild that.

Gloria Larocque Campbell Moses
(Sturgeon Lake Cree Nation, Northern Alberta)

We never learned about **Indigenous communities** in school. **My mom** never told us about our **Indigenous roots**. I spent the first **twenty-five years** of my life feeling incomplete. Now, almost twenty-five years later, I still can't help but **feel ripped off** and **angry** that **my culture** was kept from me. It feels like **someone stole** a piece of **my soul** —and I've been working ever since to get it back.

Nathalie Bertin
(Métis)

i am not your princess

A Conversation with a Massage Therapist
Francine Cunningham (Cree/Métis)

What are you?

Excuse me?

You don't look all white.

I'm Indigenous.

Oh, well what kind of Native are you?

Cree.

You don't really look it.

I am also Scottish and Métis on my dad's side.

Were you raised on a reserve?

No, I was raised in the city.

Oh, well, I guess you're not a real one then, right?

. . .

What do you do?

I'm a student.

High school upgrading?

No, I'm getting my master's degree.

Well, good thing you got the taxpayers to pay for it, right? Wish I could go to school for free.

. . .

Anyways, I guess you're one of the good ones, right?

What?

Well, you're not a drunk or anything, good for you.

. . .

Okay, turn over, let me get to your back.

Illustration by Karlene Harvey (Tsilhqot'in/Carrier/Okanagan)

We Are Not A Costume

Jessica Deer (Mohawk)

Even during a time of reconciliation, Indigenous people are faced with having to defend their identities from being mocked, used as a trend or form of entertainment every single day. The highly inaccurate and dehumanizing representations of Indigenous peoples in sports, on television, on the runway, or in costumes on the shelves of a Halloween store shape much of what people know and think about us.

While people who wear "Indian Maiden" costumes often do not have racist or harmful intentions, their actions contribute to larger challenges. We're placed in the realm of cavemen, trolls, and woodland fairies, and that affects how society understands the real social, political, and economic issues we face. Not only do these costumes paint all Indigenous people with the same Spaghetti-Western brush but, many of them also objectify, victimize, and romanticize Indigenous women and girls as an exotic other.

While someone may think they look supercute as an "Indian Princess" or as "Reservation Royalty" for a fun and harmless evening, they have the privilege of removing that costume at the end of the night.

Indigenous women and girls do not.

We have to deal with ongoing marginalization and the lingering effects of colonization, like a culture that normalizes violence against us.

That's why I spent Halloween weekend campaigning against offensive "Pocahottie" and "Indian Warrior" costumes. The goal: to plant a seed in the consciousness of more Canadians about cultural appropriation, Indigenous representations, and identity. Sometimes you have to ruffle a few neon plastic feathers to get your message out.

Illustration by Karlene Harvey (Tsilhqot'in/Carrier/Okanagan)

The Invisible Indians

Shelby Lisk (Mohawk)

Registration No
1640964701
Registry Group no. and
Name
164 –
MOHAWKS
OF THE BAY
OF QUINTE

*It's strange to me how people always want me
to be an "authentic Indian." When I say I'm
Haudenosaunee, they want me to look a certain way.
Act a certain way. They're disappointed when what
they get is . . . just me. White-faced, red-haired.
They spent hundreds of years trying to assimilate my
ancestors, trying to create Indians who could blend
in like me. But now they don't want me either. I'm
not Indian enough. They can't make up their minds.
They want buckskin and war paint, drumming,
songs in languages they can't understand recorded
for them, but with English subtitles of course. They
want educated, well-spoken, but not too smart.
Christian, well-behaved, never questioning. They
want to learn the history of the people, but not the
ones who are here now, waving signs in their faces,
asking them for clean drinking water, asking them
why their women are going missing, asking them
why their land is being ruined. They want fantastical
stories of the Indians that used to roam this land.
They want my culture behind glass in a museum.
But they don't want me. I'm not Indian enough.*

What's There to Take Back?

Tiffany Midge (Hunkpapa Lakota)

"This project seeks submissions from Native American artists, re-creating Tiger Lily to fit a real model of Indigenous womanhood . . . Many argue that we ought to eschew Tiger Lily altogether, valorizing a more authentic character. But she is still an Indian princess, the sort young girls on and off reservations across America look to as a model, having very few authentic representations of their lives in the public sphere."

Really? Young Natives need an authentic representation to look up to (eye roll)? Why would an online indie publication put out a call for submissions based on the theme of taking back Tiger Lily? Are Indian people in such dire need, at such a loss for Native American role models to look up to, so lacking in cultural heroes or icons to claim as their very own that the only solution is to exhume from the mausoleum of twentieth-century relics the Disney cartoon character Tiger Lily? She was never my model of Indigenous womanhood.

When I think of a model of Indigenous womanhood, I immediately think of my mother: a woman who lost her own mother when she was sixteen, became widowed at twenty-one with a baby girl, and no education or prospects, left the reservation, settled in Seattle, remarried, had me, divorced, raised two daughters, put in thirty years as a civil servant, and was beloved by a great many friends and family. She is my model of Indigenous womanhood.

When I think of a model of Indigenous womanhood, I also think of my grandma Eliza, a woman who grew up dirt poor, who scraped out a living, her clothes threadbare through long, cold winters spent eating the same meal for weeks, a young woman with so few choices she married a widower and raised his daughters, even though she loved another man, who she eventually did marry. She is my model of Indigenous womanhood.

Also, my grandma Charity: daughter of the first Assiniboine Presbyterian in Fort Peck, who raised several children, who steered them toward college educations, who lived to age ninety-eight, who was honored by the governor, who gave a televised speech in her original language, Dakota. She is my model of Indigenous womanhood.

My sister, my aunts, cousins . . . they were my models of Indigenous womanhood growing up. The Iroquois educator who ran the Native consortium program was my model of Indigenous womanhood. The singer Buffy Sainte-Marie was my model of Indigenous womanhood. Louise Erdrich and Joy Harjo were my models of Indigenous womanhood.

There is no "taking back," no "reclamation" of an idea that never belonged to Indians in the first place. Would anyone want to reclaim Frito Bandito? Aunt Jemima? Charlie Chan? God, no. These images are analogous to images of Tiger Lily. They are made from the same poison. The same polluted well.

Illustration by Chief Lady Bird (Anishinaabe)

Why not Indians?

"You see doctors, lawyers, fireman, everyday people played by people of all different ethnic groups these days, why not Indians, I mean we don't talk about 'Indian things' all the time, I mean, so much of our lives are lived like everyday people, why can't Hollywood reflect that?"

– Actress DeLanna Studi (Cherokee)

DeLanna Studi playing Kiona Stetson in the short film *Blessed*

STEREOTYPE THIS

MELANIE FEY (DINÉ)

Today I couldn't handle the pain of being an American Indian
There's a clawing deep inside,
Like a spider in a thirsty drought
And it screams in broken lullaby:

> *I don't want to be a drunk Indian*
> *I don't want to be the drunk Indian*

Today a boarding school sat like a lump in my throat
And the ghosts of dead Indian children
With butchered hair and broken Christian wings,
Shattered bottles down on my feet and screamed:

> *We don't want to be drunk Indians*
> *We don't want to be the drunk Indians*

Today I walked away from my lover
How do I tell him that I feel the Trail of Tears like hard sand in my veins?
That I feel Wounded Knee like a frozen battlefield in my stomach?
That I feel the Long Walk like snapping branches in my legs?
I feel it all every time I sip from another bottle of burned memories—
The residue of genocide
And it hums in broken lullaby:

> *You are a drunk Indian*
> *You are the drunk Indian*

And I feel coyote pull in my finger tips
Porcupine in my skin
Crow in my hair
My feet like broken stairs

Because history moves like a fevered heat down through the arteries of generations
Because PTSD to the family tree is like an ax
Because colonization is the ghosts of buffalos with broken backs
Because today only burning flags could be found at the ghost dance of my people

> *And they all chant in unison:*

> *We are not a stereotype*
> *We are not*
> > *Your stereotype*

Identity of Stripes and Stars by Sierra Edd (Diné) ——————

Real NDNZ

Pamela J. Peters (Navajo)

Real NDNZ Re-Take Hollywood recreates classic portraits of movie stars

of yesteryear, replacing those past film icons with contemporary Native

American actors. The idea of the relic stereotypical Indian needs to change.

Negative representations of Indians have been the norm in mass media.

Even today, films such as *The Ridiculous 6* and *The Revenant* only showcase

Indians as relics of the past, portraying Indians as obstacles to progress.

Shayna Jackson (Dakota/Cree) channeling Audrey Hepburn
Deja Jones (Eastern Shoshone) channeling Ava Gardner (next page)

I Am the Only American Indian

by Cecelia Rose La Pointe (Ojibway/Métis)

I am the only American Indian sitting at the table during lunch. It's awkward but I am used to it. There's a group of White kids over there. A group of Black kids over there. Congregation segregation. A few stragglers, weirdos, hippies, and nerds.

I congregate alone.

We are so DIVIDED by race. But I feel comfortable as an American Indian on my own. Long beaded earrings, a beaded barrette, my NAIS Native student organization bag. The beat of the drum in my soul. Ancestors all around me.

I talked to my Ojibway grandma yesterday. She's way up in the UP — the Upper Peninsula of Michigan — on the rez.

Shifting in my seat I pay close attention to the birds outside. No one else is paying attention to them. That is how city folk are. They are moving and going and walking and talking nonstop. So I tune out the loud conversations, laughter, and gossip and listen to the birds.

I adjust my long hair. I let it down, showing my pride. Sometimes us Natives see each other on campus. We might not talk but we nod as we walk by. Some Natives wear their hair long to stand out. Our hair :SHOUTS: ACTIVISM, REBELLION, and RECLAIMING OUR CULTURE, HERITAGE, and IDENTITY. It has to -SHOUT- because otherwise no one would LISTEN to us!

I've finished my lunch. I walk alone out of the dorm cafeteria. The smell of fries and other processed foods lingers in the air. I walk out the door and down the paved sidewalk to my next class. I have SURVIVED INVISIBILITY.

It **bugs me** is when people would say how all of the blonde haired, blue-eyed girls are the **prettiest girls** in school. It **makes me feel** that people **don't see me** as **beautiful**.

Hazel Hedgecoke
(Sioux/Hunkpapa/Wendat/Métis/Cherokee/Creek)

As **Indigenous women writers** and **artists** we are continually trying to exist, live, and love in a world that doesn't always show its love for us. This means, part of the artist's call is to **turn past traumas** on their heads, upside down, inside out, lift it up then put it back down as something changed and **transformed** so that others can find **something beautiful** or hopeful in it. For that beauty and hope to exist we as **Native American women** must dive headfirst into the muck, ugliness, **stark darkness** of that wreckage. This is what we do—we recast wounds in unending light. And so, **light**, **love**, and **courage** are circles we keep coming back to.

Tanaya Winder
(Duckwater Shosone)

pathfinders

When I Have a Daughter

Ntawnis Piapot (Piapot Cree Nation)

When I have a daughter . . . I'll tell her.
Don't wait. Don't whine. Don't "pine."
Go for it. Work for it. Earn it.
I'll tell her stories of my younger years.
Spilt beers, unfounded fears.
I'll hold her close as my mother did . . .
When her heart is broken, when her spirit is down.
When all the men have left and all the women have turned their backs.
And I'll cry with her . . . knowing this won't be the last time.
Knowing there's more hurt in the world that I can't protect her from.
I'll hold her up when she succeeds and hold her more when she fails.
When I have a daughter . . . I'll remind her of what happened.
Of why she never met her *kokum*. And what happened to our people.
I'll tell her grand stories of her *mushum* . . . and how he made it rain.
How he fought and sacrificed and envisioned her in this moment . . .
I'll dance with her in my arms late at night as a baby.
And imagine the beauty she'll hold as a young woman.
When I have a daughter . . . I'll tell her to never lower her standards.
That as women, our ambition and strong words scare weak-minded people.
That as much as you want to be an opinionated woman fighting for justice—
You'll be shunned.
You'll be ostracized.
You'll be labeled an emotional rebel.
Troublemaker. Truth-teller.
And I hope I'll instill enough courage for her to walk alone. And love wholeheartedly.
And laugh that Cree laugh and be proud of her features.
When I have a daughter . . . I'll name her and hold her high.
And I'll look at her as you looked at me.

Memories by Aura Last (Oneida)

Defender of Mother Earth

"Native Americans are still part of this country. People act like we're gone but we're still here."
– AnnaLee

AnnaLee Rain Yellowhammer (Hunkapapa, Standing Rock Sioux) is just thirteen years old. But she's a leader in the largest Native American protest in a century. She started a petition to stop the Dakota Access Pipeline. Originally the pipeline was to be routed near the city of Bismarck, North Dakota. People there feared a leak would pollute their drinking water so it was rerouted to the Standing Rock reservation, crossing the Missouri River twice. The Missouri is one of the main sources of drinking water for the thousands of people who live on the reservation and the millions who live farther downstream. Sacred burial sites on the Standing Rock reservation are also being destroyed in the construction of the pipeline. More than 550,000 people have signed AnnaLee's petition to stop the Dakota Access Pipeline. AnnaLee and thirty-seven other others, mostly teens from the Standing Rock Reservation, ran 2000 miles (3200 km) to Washington, DC, to hand over the petition.

I am 13 years old, and I've spent my whole life drinking and fishing from the Missouri River in North Dakota. After school, when I'm not babysitting for my auntie, I go to the One Mile Creek right below my grandma's house to fish for creek minnows. In the summer, I—like my mother and grandmother before me—go to the river to swim with friends.

As members of the Standing Rock Sioux Tribe, my family has lived here for generations. Today our lives on the reservation are still defined by the river.

But now an oil company wants to build a pipeline that will cross the river a mile away from our reservation, carrying 570,000 barrels of crude oil across each day. We're terrified that it could leak into our water, but the company doesn't seem to care.

…

Across the reservation, young people are acting as defenders of Mother Earth and saying no to Big Oil. We know that we can live without electricity, we can live without oil, but we can't live without water. No one can.

We demand "rezpect" for our water, our land, and our voices.

Portrait by Sierra Edd (Diné)

DIGITAL

Andrea Landry @AndreaLandry1 · 3 Aug 2016
The only way the issue of violence and our women will be solved is through self-responsibility, self-accountability, and self-revolution.

Lindsay Izzy Belone
@izzyb1288
⚙ 👤 Follow

#OverseasVoting #NativeVote16 #NativeVote
#ImWithHer #Hillary2016 #IVOTED ☑

12:10 AM · 20 Oct 2016

muskwamedia
16w
19 likes
muskwamedia We are missing a few more Indigenous Women in this pic. You know who you are! Love & Laughter 😊
#WhoistherealPocahontas
#tammybeauvaisdesigns

Jess Housty
@haitsukvoice
⚙ Following

You can help us bear the costs that the company won't. Please donate/share:
fundrazr.com/b1B0J3?ref=ab_...
#NathanEStewart

Jessica R. Metcalfe @beyondbuckskin · Aug 19
What do you think? Is it ever OK for a white person to wear a feather headdress? >>

Is it ever OK for a white person to wear a feather headdress?
Let's settle this once and for all.
mic.com

RETWEETS 44 LIKES 8
6:11 PM · 24 Oct 2016

Kim TallBear
@KimTallBear
⚙ Following

Good read. #NotYourMascot. The great failure of the Indians mascot debate? Thinking of it only as racism

NOT IN MY TEPEE

The great failure of the Indians mascot debate? Thinking of it only as racism
While real Indians protest in North Dakota, another protest is happening -- watching the World Series and the fake "chief" Wahoo, demonstrating how far we still have ...
espn.com

RETWEETS 138 LIKES 114

5:44 PM · 26 Oct 2016
↩ ♺ 138 ♥

Dr. Adrienne Keene ✓
@NativeApprops
So don't come at me with the "get over it" "I don't understand" "It's just a costume" "why can't I dress like an Indian??". READ. SOMETHING.
RETWEETS 16 LIKES 50
9:16 AM · 11 Oct 2016

Social media is a tool that unites global communities to take action, take notice, or take a stand. Indigenous women use Twitter, Facebook, and Instagram to inform and motivate followers and to raise funds for collective actions for the greater good. Using these platforms, they create a "digital smoke signal" that reaches out across all the nations, building community and awareness for everything from an environmental activist movement like #NoDAPL to an inspiring #MotivationMonday message.

SHONI SCHIMMEL (UMATILLA) WNBA STAR

"My mom had a huge impact on my life. She instilled it into our brains that 'it's not about you, it's about all the other Native Americans out there who don't get the chance and who may not have the same confidence in themselves that you have.'"

LIVING THEIR DREAMS

SEPTEMBER BIG CROW
(TSUU T'INA NATION)
GOLFER AND MARTIAL ARTS STAR

"For eighteen years, I was in an abusive relationship. One day I had the courage to get up and leave. I started to join programs like martial arts and boot camps.

That saved my life. Instead of turning to substances, from living in fear and being traumatized for years, I gained confidence and strength with workouts and my love of golf."

"I want to be an example of someone who believes that setting goals, working hard, and never giving up does pay off and that your dreams can come true. Native youth inspire me. I want them to know I am carrying Native America in my heart."

ASHTON LOCKLEAR (LUMBEE)
OLYMPIC GYMNAST

BRIGITTE LACQUETTE (OJIBWE)
U OF MINNESOTA AND CANADIAN
NATIONAL TEAM HOCKEY PLAYER

"I grew up in a small town and I played with Métis kids, Aboriginal kids—it was great. Then I started going to the bigger cities like Winnipeg, and racist stuff started happening. At one hockey tournament, a girl called me a 'dirty indian' and told me to 'go back to your reserve.'

I got really emotional and started crying. My dad told me, 'Beat them on the ice. Be the bigger person.'"

Good Medicine
Interview with JANET SMYLIE (Cree/Métis)

When did you decide to study medicine?
I've always been interested in science. I was a curious kid. My father, who is of mixed European ancestry (Irish, Scottish, and English), trained as a geophysicist, so he was a university professor. My mom was a nurse, one of the few Métis women who was trained as a nurse in her time. I had a lot of educational opportunities. My parents encouraged my scientific curiosity. My father taught me to respect my intelligence and that I was good at math. That's the ace up my sleeve. Thanks to my dad I'm not afraid of middle-aged white guys.

What was your life like growing up?
Unlike my mother, I didn't get teased or called half-breed when I was growing up. I lived north of Toronto and there were no other Métis people around besides my family. I lost my mom to cancer when I was thirteen. So as a grieving thirteen-year-old girl, I just wanted to drink myself into a stupor. School was a bit of a refuge for me. That helped because drinking was only a weekend thing. Drinking led to a whole bunch of other traumatic experiences. Luckily I was living in a rural area where I had lots of kind friends trying to look out for me, but there were still challenges, sexual assaults. Different place, different time, no supports, I wouldn't be here. I would be one of the Missing and Murdered Indigenous Women.

How did you change the destructive path you were on?
I think what got me out of it was linking up with the local Ontario Native Women's Association and some other Indigenous community role models. I began to do a little bit of traditional ceremony and get a little bit involved in getting cultural teachings. That was scary too. At one of my first big gatherings, a Cree knowledge keeper had been invited. I'm Cree/Métis and was so happy I could be the helper. Of course, I didn't know how to be a very good helper. I felt ashamed.

What challenges did you face in becoming a doctor?
I was a mixed-blood Indigenous woman who was struggling in medical school. I was still binge drinking and being this party girl and was quite promiscuous. I finally got confronted with my grief for my mom in anatomy class. At that time we had to take the boxes of bones home. A box of bones. It was someone. I became aware of the connection between body and spirit. I couldn't deal with working on the cadavers. Our anatomy lab was on Friday, so I'd binge drink on Thursday night so I'd be going into the anatomy lab in a fog.

I took a leave from medical school. I was still doing fine academically but I was having some depression. It's common and I'm very lucky that I have been able to get treatment and support. For me, it's something that I have to deal with. It's like any other kind of chronic illness. I have to be alert and manage and do self care.

My grandmother was in Saskatoon and I spent quite a bit of time visiting her. She was an archetypal Métis Grandma who was born in 1918 and survived. Thank goodness I had my grandmother. There were a lot of people in the Métis community who were very generous, kind of adopting me, taking me under their wing. I really believe that if you look, the person that you need to help you will be there if you're open to it.

How did connecting with your Métis culture impact your life?
Starting to understand who I was as an Indigenous woman really helped me. As soon as I stopped drinking, I figured out that I preferred to have female sexual partners over male. I was gay, and I think that might have been part of the hiding with alcohol. My mom, my bio mom, had gone through a lot as a kid, we think. She made a real effort to give us books on how our bodies worked and about being careful about getting pregnant. Still, I never valued my sexuality, not recognizing that it was a valuable, sacred thing. Finding out who I was as an Indigenous woman and being able to connect to that and get cultural teachings and start to access spirituality was really an important way to get out of that pattern of self-harm.

You've done a lot of research on how unintentional racism by health practitioners impacts the care indigenous people receive. What have you learned?

We all have race bias. If you actually look at the evidence—the evidence being from Indigenous knowledge keepers and knowledge from highfalutin Harvard scientists—we have race bias. And we don't know why. People might say it's socialized or developmental biology. But we look at people and we notice if they look like us or are different from us and then we start to treat the people that look like us better. It is a huge weakness of human beings. The problem in Canada is we pretend it doesn't exist but it does. For Indigenous peoples or self-reflective people, or people of color, it's no news. We know it exists. It's just the white people who are surprised. You need to support people in getting to a place where they can sit with their discomfort honestly and learn from it. And that's a big job! I know what a big job it was for me growing up. My lens got distorted by internalized racism.

Illustration by Chief Lady Bird (Anishinaabe)

More Than Meets the Eye

ReMatriate takes back Indigenous female identity

ReMATRIATE™
we have masters degrees in architecture

"We're trying to capture the breadth of the number of distinct Indigenous cultures that actually exist in North America–from the urban Indigenous to extremely rural communities. There's a huge variety of lived experiences among Indigenous peoples. We're not a token image; we're from very vast cultures over a massive land base."

~ Collective founding member, architect Kelly Edzerza–Bapty (Tahltan of the Stikine River and Headwaters)

ReMATRIATE™

ReMATRIATE™
we are scholars and theorists

ReMATRIATE

ndigenous women are taking control of how they and their traditions are seen. A group of Indigenous women formed the collective ReMatriate to show the world that Indigenous women are not a single stereotyped image; that they hold multiple identities and are much more than meets the eye.

The name ReMatriate was chosen to communicate their vision to take back Indigenous female identity and a traditional space in society, to honor the role of the Matriarch in their communities. This diverse group of volunteers shares images through social media to shatter stereotypes of Native women.

REMATRIATE™
we are strengthening our relationships with each other and the land

REMATRIATE™
we are prioritizing Indigenous ways of being

Eliza Archie

REMATRIATE
we are inspired by our elders

REMATRIATE
we are tech here

REMATRIATE
We are resilient, creative and use art as a tool to tell important stories, to speak our truths

"We aren't historic figures; we are modern women. Some of us are academics, some of us are lawyers, some of us are architects, and yet we all continue to practice our culture in different ways, whether it's weaving or dancing or hunting or tanning hides. We just wanted to show the complexity of our identities, and how we've incorporated traditions into our modern life."

~ Collective founding member, lawyer Claire Anderson (Taku River Tlingit First Nation)

REMATRIATE™
We are strong women

OTTA-MUSTA

BABY-GIRLZ-GOTTA-MUSTANG

Dana Claxton (Hunkpapa Lakota)

WHEN YOU THINK OF INDIGENOUS GIRLS WHAT DO YOU SEE?

I see deep NDN beauty.

I see powerful and knowledgeable girls who have the enormous potential to lead us into a just future. I see girls who thrive and survive despite the violence of colonialism and settler colonialism. I see girls who endure lateral violence. I see girls who are smart. I see girls who need to know history. I see girls who continue to teach me what it means to be an NDN woman. What does it mean to be an NDN woman? To me it means to care for your family and community with generosity, courage, wisdom, and fortitude.

— Dana Claxton

"DEAR PAST SELF"

by Isabella Fillspipe (Oglala Lakota)

Dear Past Self,
My advice to you is
Please don't ever sit in your room and lock yourself
away because you don't think you're good enough.

Because you will never influence the world trying to be like it.
You will get sad, I'm not going to lie.
But life is sad, beautiful and everything in between.
I want you to live and not just survive.
And I know loving yourself is hard,
But here's the thing
You are loved
You are worthy of love and respect
And you can be loved,
Even on the days when you believe you are nothing.

People will come and go
Some are cigarette breaks
Others are forest fires.
And not everything you lose is a loss
I also need you to remember that:

You are allowed to cry
You are allowed to scream
But you are not allowed to give up.

If you ever need a hero
Become one.
And for the sake of your own life
If you have something to say
Say it. Life is too short to sit in silence
And stop trying to please other people
You will be much happier if you would stop caring what they think.
I know it's hard
But it's time you were comfortable in your own skin
Everything is happening as it is supposed to
With hidden blessings that you will soon understand
And whatever happens, remember,
I did, I do, and I will always

Love you.

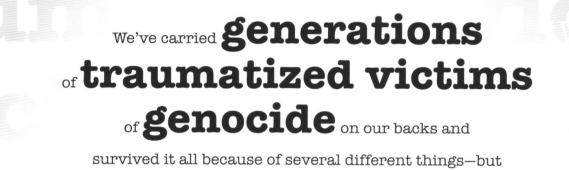

We've carried **generations** of **traumatized victims** of **genocide** on our backs and survived it all because of several different things—but **one of our tools is humor.** **We Native women** are very funny. The **world doesn't know** it but **they should**.

Adrianne Chalepah
(Kiowa/Apache)

We must and will have **women leaders** among us. **Native women** are going to **raise the roof** and **decry** the dirty house which **patriarchy** and **racism** have built on our backs.

Lee Maracle
(Stó:lō Nation)

LITTLE SISTER

Tasha Spillett (Cree)

Little sister
I see you even if you have yet to see
yourself
even if you mask yourself in fragments of
untruths of you
even when you cloak yourself because
somewhere, sometime, someone has made
you feel that to hide is safer than to
shine as you were meant to do

Little sister
I wish I could speak into your mind
sacred words of you so loudly that they
are like the Thunderbirds when they come
to visit and wash everything away
I wish to make you a crown of sage to
show to all that rest their eyes on you,
that you are made of medicine and of
Royalty

Little sister
I will sing songs to you until your voice
remembers it was meant to dance
I will pray into being all that is needed to
remind you that you are where beauty and
strength come together to embrace
I will dance medicine into the path that
we walk on so that it is again safe for you

Little sister
I see you

Illustration by Julie Flett (Cree/Métis) ————

CONTRIBUTORS

Aza Erdrich Abe is a Turtle Mountain Ojibwe artist. Her work has shown at galleries in North Dakota, Arizona, and Minnesota. In addition to her fine art practice, Aza designs book covers for her mother, Louise Erdrich. She lives in Minneapolis with her husband, son, and two dogs.

Claire Anderson is a Taku River Tlinglit lawyer from the northern community of Atlin, British Columbia. Anderson now lives in Whitehorse, Yukon, where she practices corporate-commercial law, real estate law, will and estate law, and Aboriginal law. She is a founding member of the ReMatriate Collective.

Joanne Arnott is a Métis/mixed-blood author of six books of poetry and three books in other genres. She is currently poetry editor for *EVENT magazine.*

Monique Bedard (Aura Last) is a Haudenosaunee (Oneida) artist, workshop facilitator, and muralist who grew up in a small town in southern Ontario. In 2010, she earned a BFA from the University of Lethbridge. She is currently living in Tkaronto and completing a major project at the Toronto Art Therapy Institute titled "Our Stories Our Truths: An Art-Based Storytelling Project."

Gwen Benaway is of Anishinaabe and Métis descent. Her first collection of poetry, *Ceremonies for the Dead*, was published in 2013 and her second collection, *Passage,* in 2016, both by Kegedonce Press.

Nathalie Bertin is a Franco-Métis artist and educator from Toronto, Ontario. Bertin's Indigenous ancestry and her relationship with the environment play a central role in her life and work. She shares their teachings and worldview to empower others and to help bridge the gap between Indigenous and non-Indigenous people.

September Big Crow (Tsuu T'ina Nation) is a golfer and martial arts athlete. She works as a coordinator for a family/domestic violence program for Aboriginal communities. Her goal is to become the first Tsuu T'ina woman to receive her black belt.

Maria Campbell (Métis) is best known for her important memoir, *Halfbreed*, which initiated a rebirth of Aboriginal literature in Canada. She is a great-grandmother, Elder, author, playwright, and filmmaker.

Tenille Campbell (Dene/Métis) is a photographer, blogger, writer, single mother, and student at the University of Saskatchewan. Her PhD thesis is focused on family stories and kinship in her home community of English River First Nation. She can be found drinking coffee and hiding in the background of social events.

Imajyn Cardinal (Cree/Dene) started acting at the age of seven. She is the daughter of Gemini award-winning actress Michelle Thrush. In 2015, she starred in *The Saver* in her first lead role.

Adrianne Chalepah (Kiowa/Apache) is an entertainer from Anadarko, Oklahoma. Passionate about Indigenous/female empowerment, she formed the world's only all-female, all-Native American comedy group, Ladies of Native Comedy. Adrianne is a mother of three, wife, and businesswoman.

Lianne Marie Leda Charlie is a descendant of the Tagé Cho Hudän (Big River People), Northern Tutchone-speaking people of the Yukon. She is a political science instructor at Yukon College and a PhD candidate at the University of Hawai`i at Mānoa. @littlesalmonwoman

Chief Lady Bird (Nancy King) is a Potawatomi and Chippewa artist from Rama First Nation with paternal ties to Moose Deer Point. She makes art under her Anishinaabe name *Ogimaa Kwe Bnes* (Chief Lady Bird). Having completed a BFA at OCAD University, Chief Lady Bird works as a freelance muralist, street artist, illustrator, and designer. Instagram: @chiefladybird

Dana Claxton (Hunkpapa Lakota) is a critically acclaimed artist. She investigates beauty, the sociopolitical, and the spiritual. Her work is held in public and private collections. Her paternal Euro-grandmother taught her to harvest/preserve food and her maternal Lakota grandmother to seek justice. Dana is an associate professor at the University of British Columbia.

Clear Wind Blows Over the Moon is a Cree First Nations healer, poet, writer, big drum keeper, artist, intergenerational Indian Residential School survivor, and spiritual/environmental activist. She writes poetry to transcend her painful past and to give voice to Indigenous women and the innocent children that didn't survive. clearwindblowsoverthemoon.wordpress.com / @indigorave

Francine Cunningham (Cree/Métis) is a writer, artist, and educator. Her creative nonfiction has appeared in *The Malahat Review* and in the anthology *Boobs*, published by Caitlin Press. Her fiction and poetry have appeared in *The Puritan, Echolocation Magazine*, *The Maynard*, and more. She is a graduate of the UBC Creative Writing MFA program. francinecunningham.ca.

Danielle Daniel is the author and illustrator of *Sometimes I Feel Like a Fox*, winner of the Marilyn Baillie Picture Book Award, a finalist for the First Nation Communities Read Award and the Blue Spruce Award. Her second children's book *Once in a Blue Moon* is forthcoming. Danielle is Métis and she writes and paints in Sudbury, Ontario.

Jessica Deer is a Kanien'kehá:ka (Mohawk) journalist and youth leader from Kahnawà:ke, Quebec.

Rosanna Deerchild (Cree) is the host of *Unreserved* on CBC Radio One. She is an award-winning Cree author and has been a broadcaster for almost twenty years—including stints with APTN, CBC Radio, Global, and a variety of Indigenous newspapers. She hails from O-Pipon-Na-Piwin Cree Nation, Manitoba.

Sierra Edd (Diné) is a poet, filmmaker, and artist. She is a student at Brown University, concentrating in ethnic studies. Her work engages with historical narraties and the experience of being a Diné woman by challenging colonialism and striving to empower the voices of young Native women

Kelly Edzerza-Bapty is an architect from the Tahltan Nation of Telegraph Creek and one of the founders of the ReMatriate Collective. She has a Master of Architecture degree from the University of British Columbia and is the second woman of First Nations descent to graduate from this program.

Ka'ila Farrell-Smith is a contemporary Klamath/Modoc visual artist based in Portland, Oregon. She works as an adjunct professor in Indigenous Nations Studies at Portland State University and is co-director for the *Signal Fire* Artist and Creative Agitator residency program.

Melanie Fey is a Diné writer, zinester, and Indigenous feminist. She was spawned in Tuba City, Arizona, but currently resides in Portland, Oregon, where she works as a public library minion. Her work explores the Indigenous diaspora, celebrating the LGBTQ/Two-Spirit community and questioning the dichotomy of being mixed race.

Isabella Fillspipe (Oglala Lakota) is a student at Red Cloud High School on the Pine Ridge Indian Reservation in South Dakota. She plans to pursue a degree in cultural anthropology, but is also hoping to pursue writing.

Julie Flett (Cree/Métis) is an award-winning author, illustrator, and artist currently living in Vancouver, BC. She received the Aboriginal Literature Award for her book *Wild Berries/Pakwa che Menisu* (2014) and was nominated for the Governor General's Award for Children's Literature for her book *Owls See Clearly at Night: A Michif Alphabet* (L'alphabet di Michif) in 2010.

Nahanni Fontaine (Anishinaabe) is a member of the Legislative Assembly of Manitoba. Before entering politics, Nahanni worked as Special Advisor on Aboriginal Women's Issues for the Indigenous Issues Committee of the Cabinet of Manitoba, with a focus on Missing and Murdered Indigenous Women and Girls.

Karlene Harvey is an illustrator, artist, and writer who lives in Vancouver, BC. Her passion for arts-based publishing began with a love for graphic novels and zines. She is from the Tsilhqot'in, Carrier, and Okanagan nations and grew up in the Lower Mainland of British Columbia.

Hazel Hedgecoke (Sioux/Hunkpapa/Wendat/Métis/Cherokee/Creek) is a high school student.

Rayna Hernandez (Lakota) was born in Yankton, South Dakota, and raised in Gayville, SD by her mother, who continually encouraged her to pursue her interest in the arts. In her undergraduate studies, Rayna has been investigating the concept of identity hybridity in relation to her Indigenous bloodlines and her westernized upbringing.

Linda Hogan (Chickasaw) is an internationally recognized public speaker and writer of poetry, fiction, and essays. She is a professor emerita, University of Colorado and was writer in residence for the Chickasaw Nation.

Wakeah Jhane is a self-taught ledger artist from the Penatuka and Yaparucah bands of Comanche, and is also Blackfeet and Kiowa.

Helen Knott is Dane Zaa and Nehiyawak from the Prophet River First Nation in British Columbia. Helen is an activist and poet-writer working for Indigenous land rights in Canada.

Brigitte Lacquette (Ojibwe, Cote First Nation) is a hockey player who plays defense for the University of Minnesota Duluth and the Canadian Women's National Hockey team. She played for Team Canada at each of the last two World Championships, winning silver medals at both.

Winona LaDuke (Anishinaabe/Ojibwe) is an internationally renowned activist and environmentalist. She lives and works on the White Earth Reservation in northern Minnesota, and is a two-time vice presidential candidate with Ralph Nader for the Green Party.

Cecelia Rose LaPointe is Ojibway/Métis who is a part of Kchiwiikwedong (Keweenaw Bay Indian Community, Michigan) and is *ajijaak* (crane) clan. Cecelia is a poet and writer published in anthologies, chapbooks, dissertations, journals, magazines, and online Indigenous-Native publications. She is the owner of Red Circle Consulting and Waub Ajijaak Press.

Gloria Larocque Campbell Moses (Sturgeon Lake Cree Nation, Northern Alberta) is an artist and activist. Her Aboriginal Angel Doll Project inspired the Native Women's Association of Canada's Faceless Doll Project to raise awareness about Missing and Murdered Indigenous Women and Girls.

Winona Linn (Meskwaki) is a poet, printmaker, and illustrator. Her work has appeared in numerous publications, and she has performed her spoken-word poetry in six countries on three continents. Winona lives in Paris, where she is working on her third book, a graphic novel.

Shelby Lisk (Tyendinaga Mohawk Nation) is an artist working in photography, video, and installation. Her work has been exhibited in Ottawa, Toronto, and Chicago. Shelby recently graduated from the University of Ottawa with a bachelor of fine arts with a minor in women's studies.

Ashton Locklear (Lumbee) is an artistic gymnast from North Carolina. She is a 2014 World team gold medalist, a member of the US national team, and an alternate on the Olympic team.

Darian Lonechild (White Bear First Nation) is a Cree/Saulteaux woman from the White Bear First Nation in Treaty 4 Territory. She is a model who has had the opportunity to work internationally throughout her life. Darian is a student at the University of Saskatchewan, pursuing an undergraduate degree in Indigenous Studies and Political Studies.

Lee Maracle (Stó:lō Nation) is a grandmother of four and mother of four who was born in North Vancouver, British Columbia. Ms. Maracle is a both an award-winning author and teacher. She is currently Mentor for Aboriginal Students at the University of Toronto and the Traditional Cultural Director for the Indigenous Theatre School.

Madelaine McCallum (Cree/Métis) is a professional dancer, model, actress, artist, and choreographer. Despite the challenges of her youth, Madelaine completed high school with honors. After her post-secondary education, she became an aboriginal youth facilitator, and continues to provide education on suicide prevention, healthy relationships, and honoring "the Fire Within."

Tiffany Midge is a humor columnist for Indian Country Today Media Network and an award-winning poet. She is Hunkpapa Lakota and allergic to horses.

Saige Mukash is a Cree artist based in Whapmagoostui, Quebec.

Pamela J. Peters (Navajo) is a multimedia documentarian photographer. Her work has been featured in *Los Angeles magazine*, *Indian Country Today Media Network*, and *Reuters*. Her work has been exhibited at venues including These Days gallery, Venice Arts gallery, and the Los Angeles Center of Photography. tachiiniiphotography.com

Ntawnis Piapot (Nehiyaw Iskwew) is from the Piapot Cree Nation in Saskatchewan. She is an award-winning journalist, a storyteller, and relative. Ntawnis strives to tell stories that affect Indigenous people across Turtle Island. The poem included is dedicated to her late mother, Elvina Piapot, *kokum* Lillian, and all other matriarchs.

Natanya Ann Pulley is a Diné (Navajo) writer and an assistant professor in the English department at Colorado College. She teaches creative writing, Native American literature, and experimental/innovative fiction. She and her husband and two dogs love living near the mountains. gappsbasement.com

Zondra (Zoey) Roy (Cree/Dene/Métis) is a poet, performing artist, community-based educator, aspiring filmmaker, and community engagement consultant. She is a recent graduate of the Saskatchewan Urban Native Teacher Education Program at the University of Saskatchewan. She has a passion for storytelling and believes that the legacy lives within the process. zoeyroy.com

Shoni Schimmel (Umatilla) is a professional basketball player for the New York Liberty team in the Women's National Basketball Association (WNBA). She was an All-American college player at the University of Louisville and a first-round draft pick of the WNBA's Atlanta Dream.

Leanne Betasmosake Simpson is a renowned Michi Saagiig Nishnaabeg scholar, writer, and artist. Working for over a decade as an independent scholar using Nishnaabeg intellectual practices, Leanne has lectured and taught extensively at universities across Canada. As a writer, Leanne was named the inaugural RBC Charles Taylor Emerging writer by Thomas King. Leanne is also a musician who combines poetry, storytelling, songwriting, and performance. She is a member of Alderville First Nation.

Janet Smylie (Cree/Métis) is a respected international leader in the field of Indigenous health. One of Canada's first Métis physicians, she has spent her twenty-five-year career focused on addressing inequities in the health of Indigenous peoples in Canada. In 2015, Smylie was named a Top 20 Pioneer of Family Medicine Research by the Canadian College of Family Physicians.

Tasha Spillett is a Cree/Trinidadian woman with a master's degree in Indigenous land-based education. She teaches for both the University of Manitoba (Native Studies) and the University of Winnipeg (Faculty of Education).

Patty Stonefish (Lakota/German/Russian/French/Polish/Mexican/HUMAN) has over a decade of martial arts experience, which she has utilized to change the way women's SELF-Defense is applied. She lives with her husband, two dogs, and three cats in Fargo, North Dakota.

DeLanna Studi (Cherokee) is an award-winning actor who works in television, film, and theater. She is the chair of the Screen Actors Guild/American Federation of Television Radio Artists (SAG-AFTRA) National Native Americans Committee.

Jen VanStrander (Western Band of Cherokee) is a second-year college student at Rochester Institute of Technology. She is involved with her school's Native American Student Association (NASA) and is president of RIT's chapter of the American Indian Science and Engineering Society (AISES).

Tania Willard (Secwepemc Nation) is an artist, graphic designer, and curator. Working within ideas about site-specific and Indigenous-led models of inclusion at BUSH gallery, her work attempts to reimagine how we enact art and culture as interconnected systems.

Tanaya Winder is an entrepreneur, motivational speaker, and performance poet from the Southern Ute, Shoshone, and Paiute Nations. She graduated from Stanford University and published her first book, *Words Like Love*, in 2015. Tanaya founded Dream Warriors, an Indigenous artist management company and created the *Sing Our Rivers Red* traveling earring exhibit to raise awareness about Missing and Murdered Indigenous Women and Girls.

AnnaLee Rain Yellowhammer (Hunkpapa/Standing Rock Sioux) is a student at Standing Rock Community High School in Fort Yates, North Dakota.

CREDITS

Cover photo by Sweetmoon Photography/Tenille Campbell, sweetmoonphotography.ca. Thanks to cover model Darian Lonechild (Cree/Saulteaux)

p.5   Epigraph by Leanne Betasamosake Simpson from an interview on *Chart Attack*. chartattack.com/news/2016/08/30/premiere-leanne-betasamosake-simpson-under-your-always-light/

p.9   Quote by Wilma Mankiller from *Mankiller: A Chief and Her People* by Wilma Pearl Mankiller with Michael Wallis. © 1993 by Wilma Mankiller and Michael Wallis, St. Martin's Press, 2000

p.16   "Blankets of Shame" excerpted from *Halfbreed* by Maria Campbell. Copyright © 1973 Maria Campbell. Reprinted by permission of McClelland & Stewart, a division of Penguin Random House Canada Limited.

p.19   "two braids" reprinted from *Calling Down the Sky* by Rosanna Deerchild, Bookland Press, 2015

p 20–21 Photo of residential school children, Cross Lake, Manitoba, 1940: Canada. Dept. Indian and Northern Affairs / Library and Archives Canada / e011080274; Photo of family courtesy of Madelaine McCallum

p.30-31 Artwork by Sierra Edd

p.32   Quote by Winona LaDuke from *Winona LaDuke: Education of a Fighter*, Jennifer H. Arlen, *The Harvard Crimson*, Nov. 10, 1980, thecrimson.com/article/1980/11/10/winona-laduke-pithe-energy-shortage-of/

p.38   Image courtesy of Prospector Films, from the feature film *The Saver*, photo by Susan Moss

p.40   "she is riding" reprinted from *Night for the Lady* by Joanne Arnott, Ronsdale Press, 2013

p.42   Dana Claxton's *Onto the Red Road* from the Collection of the Eiteljorg Museum of American Indians and Western Art

p.46, 49 Portraits by Sweetmoon Photography/Tenille Campbell. sweetmoonphotography.ca

p.50-51 Artwork by Sierra Edd

p.61   Adapted from "Why your one day as a 'sexy Indian Maiden' is dehumanizing," Opinion piece, Jessica Deer, *The Globe and Mail*, Monday, October 31, 2016

p.63-64 *The Invisible Indians* series by Shelby Lisk. Chenoa Cassidy-Matthews (Sachigo Lake First Nation), Waverly Albert (Mikisew Cree First Nation)

p.67   Adapted from "What's There to Take Back," Tiffany Midge, *Sovereign Bodies*, June 16, 2015, sovereignbodies.com/blog/whats-there-to-take-back

p.68-69 Image courtesy of Through the Wilderness Production from the short film *Blessed*, photo by John Orphan

p.72-75 *Real NDNZ* series copyright 2016, Pamela J. Peters. Deja Jones (Eastern Shoshone) channeling Ava Gardner, Shayna Jackson (Dakota/Cree) channeling Audrey Hepburn

p.76-77 Artwork by Sierra Edd

p.82   *Memories* by Monique (Aura Last) Bedard//Haudenosaunee/artist, workshop facilitator and muralist, auralast.wix.com/auralast/@auralast

p.85   Petition text from change.org, change.org/p/6814883/u/16582268

p.88   Photo of Shoni Schimmel © Cal Sport Media / Alamy Stock Photo; Quote from Indian Country Media Network, "Shoni Schimmel on NY Trade: 'A New Start, Excited to Be Here,'" Vincent Schilling, May 5, 2016

p.89   Photo of September Big Crow by Sam Svay, svayphotography.zenfolio.com, compliments of First Nation Athletics, FirstNationAthletics.com

p.90   Photo of Ashton Locklear © Amy Sanderson/ZUMA Wire/Alamy Live News; Quote taken from "Ashton Locklear (Lumbee Tribe) Excited to Be a Member of the USA Olympic Gynmnastics Team," Charlie Perry, NDNSports.com, August 5, 2016, ndnsports.com/ashton-locklear-lumbee-tribe-excited-to-be-a-member-of-the-usa-olympic-gymnastics-team/

p.91   Photo of Brigitte Lacquette © Joel Ford

p.94-95 Photos courtesy of ReMatriate and contributors, www.rematriate.com, @ReMatriate. Thanks to Kelly Edzerza-Bapty (Tahitan), Amanda Vick (Gitxsan), Anna McKenzie (Cree), Raven Anne Potschka (Haida/Métis/Mohawk), Nadya Kwandibens (Ojibwe), Andrea Landry (Anishinaabe), Amanda Strong (Métis), Grace Dove (Secwepemc), Scalia Joseph (Sḵwx̱wú7mesh/Nanaimo), Claire Anderson (Tlingit)

p.98-99 Artwork by Sierra Edd

ACKNOWLEDGMENTS

Thank you to all the contributors for sharing pieces of your hearts, baring your souls, and being brave enough to speak your truths. We're also grateful to the people who submitted material whose words and pictures don't appear on these pages. Your insights were very valuable and contributed to our deepening understanding of the issues impacting Indigenous women and girls. Your work was a huge inspiration and source of guidance throughout the development process.

A special thanks to Sierra Edd for contributing her beautiful and heartfelt illustration work for the "visual scrapbooks," and to Tenille Campbell of Sweetmoon Photography for sharing her work to help create a powerful book cover and to Darian Lonechild for the stunning shoot. Another big *miigwetch* to Inti Amaratsu for being so patient and creating yet another stunningly beautiful book—you are truly a blessing!

Thank you to the team at Annick Press for your support and for sharing our vision on the importance of this project.

And finally, Lisa would like to thank some of the amazingly powerful Indigenous women who've inspired her with their strength, resilience, and graciousness over the years:

Thank you to my mother, Pahan Pte San Win; my sister, Terrina Chretien Brace; Cindy Blackstock; Holly Fortier; Kim Tallbear; Waneek Horn-Miller; Connie Walker; Marilyn Dumont; Holly Cooper; Diane Carriere; Cherie Brant; Natiea Vinson; Neegan Aaswaakshin; Chantelle Bellrichard; Bailey Redfern; Irene Bedard; Jennifer Podesmki; Lisa Jackson; DeLanna Studi; Sarah Podemski; Grace Syme; Kinnie Starr; Shoshona Kish; Summer Garcia; Bethany Yellowtail; Sho Sho Esquiro; Linsay Willier; Sage Paul; and so many others who've been beautiful souls shining on Mother Earth.

Sechanalyagh!

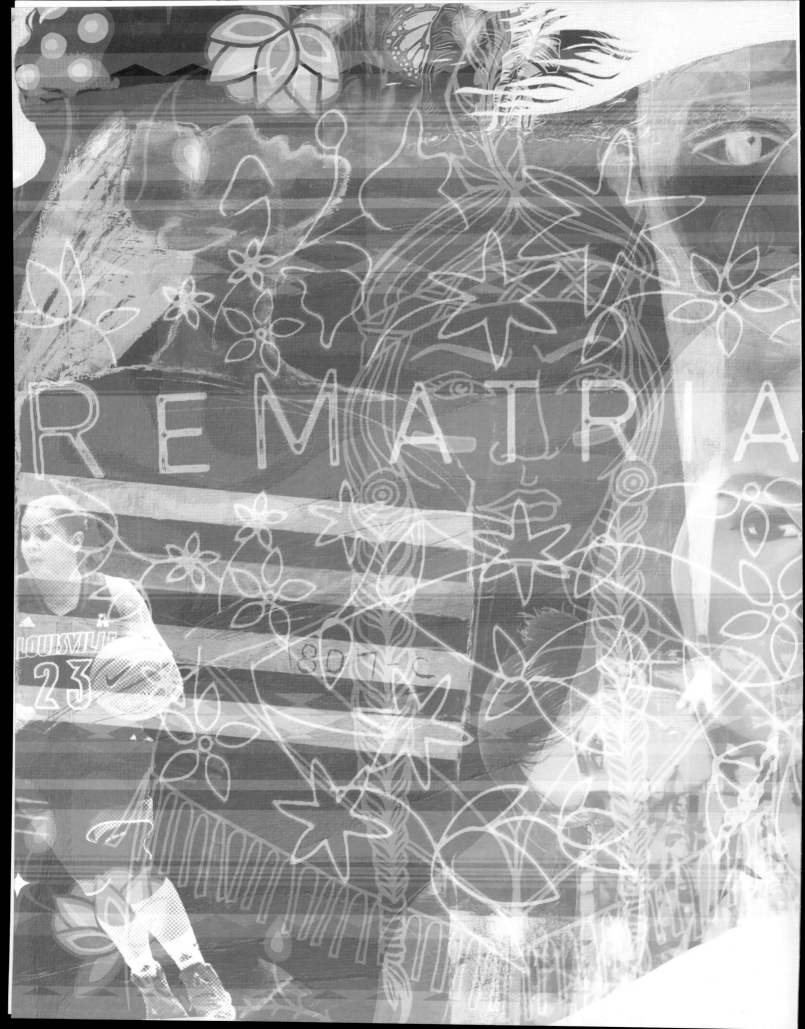